This book belongs to

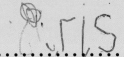 Iris

Educational consultant for I'm Ready for School: Geraldine Taylor
Phonics consultant for I'm Ready for Phonics: Kate Ruttle

Published by Ladybird Books Ltd
A Penguin Company
Penguin Books Ltd, 80 Strand, London WC2R ORL, UK
Penguin Books Australia Ltd, 707 Collins Street, Melbourne, Victoria 3008, Australia
Penguin Group (NZ) 67 Apollo Drive, Rosedale, North Shore 0632, New Zealand

001

ISBN: 978-0-72329-686-7

Printed in China

I'm Ready...
for School!

Contents

I'm Ready... for School!

I'm Ready... for Phonics!

I'm Ready... to Sing!

I'm Ready... for School!

Written by Amanda Li
Illustrated by Sonia Esplugas

My Brilliant Body

Your body is made up of lots of parts
that work together.

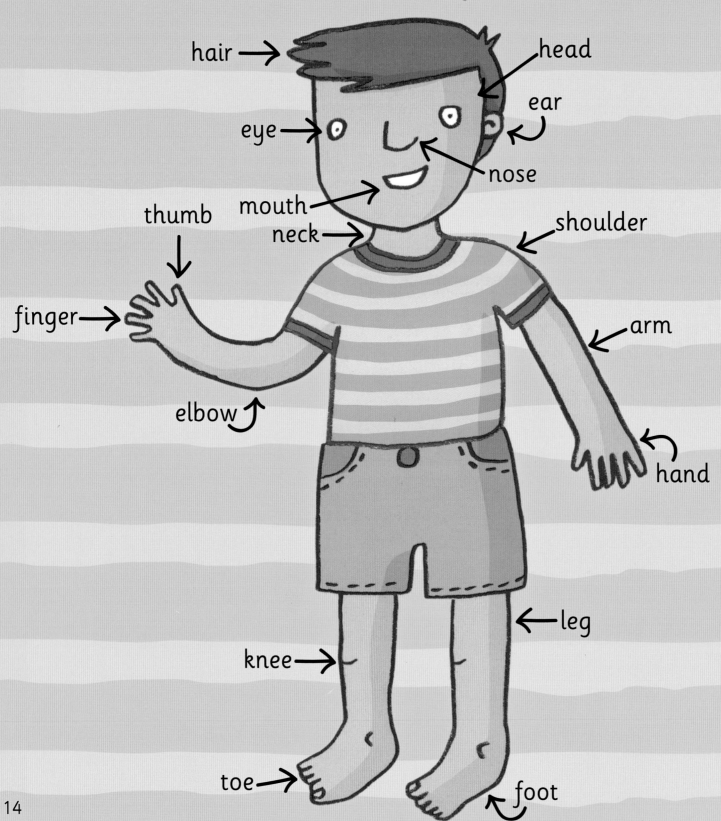

hair →

head

ear

eye →

nose

mouth

thumb

shoulder

neck →

finger →

arm

elbow ↑

hand

← leg

knee →

toe →

foot

Here are some of the things the body can do.

skip

hop

run

catch

stomp

dance

throw

jump

clap

What do you like to do?

Let's Get Dressed

Lots of clothes are drying on the washing lines.

socks

skirt

dress

t-shirt

woolly hat

belt

shoes

gloves

cardigan

flip-flops

shorts

coat

jumper

wellies

tights

sun hat

trousers

raincoat

scarf

All About Me

Can you
put on
your coat?

Can you
do up
a button?

Can you
put on
your shoes?

Can you
do up
a zip?

Point to the clothes you would wear on:

a hot day   a rainy day   a cold day

My Marvellous Manners

Being polite and having good manners
is important.

"You can use my pencil."

I can share

"Please may I have the hoop?"

I can say please

"Thank you for my present."

I can say thank you

"I like to tidy my things away."

I can tidy up

"I'm listening."

I can listen

"It's Isabel's turn first."

I can take turns

"Sorry I knocked you over."

I can say sorry

"Excuse me, may I have a go?"

I can say excuse me

Always remember to say please and thank you.

People Who Help Us

Point to the pictures. Do you know what jobs these people do?

chef

librarian

nurse

shopkeeper

builder

astronaut

doctor

firefighter

police officer

vet

teacher

farmer

What do you want to be when you grow up?

My Favourite Food

Point to the pictures and name
the different foods.

banana

orange

grapes

yoghurt

milk

bread

peas

carrot

sweetcorn

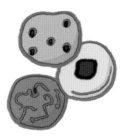

biscuits

pizza

cheese

What is your favourite food?

 apple

 chips

 water

 egg

 cucumber

 tomato

 potato

 strawberry

 fish fingers

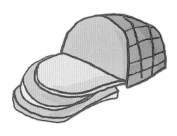 ham

 orange juice

 sandwich

Things That Go

Point to the pictures and name the different vehicles you can see.

helicopter

bicycle

motorbike

bus

car

24

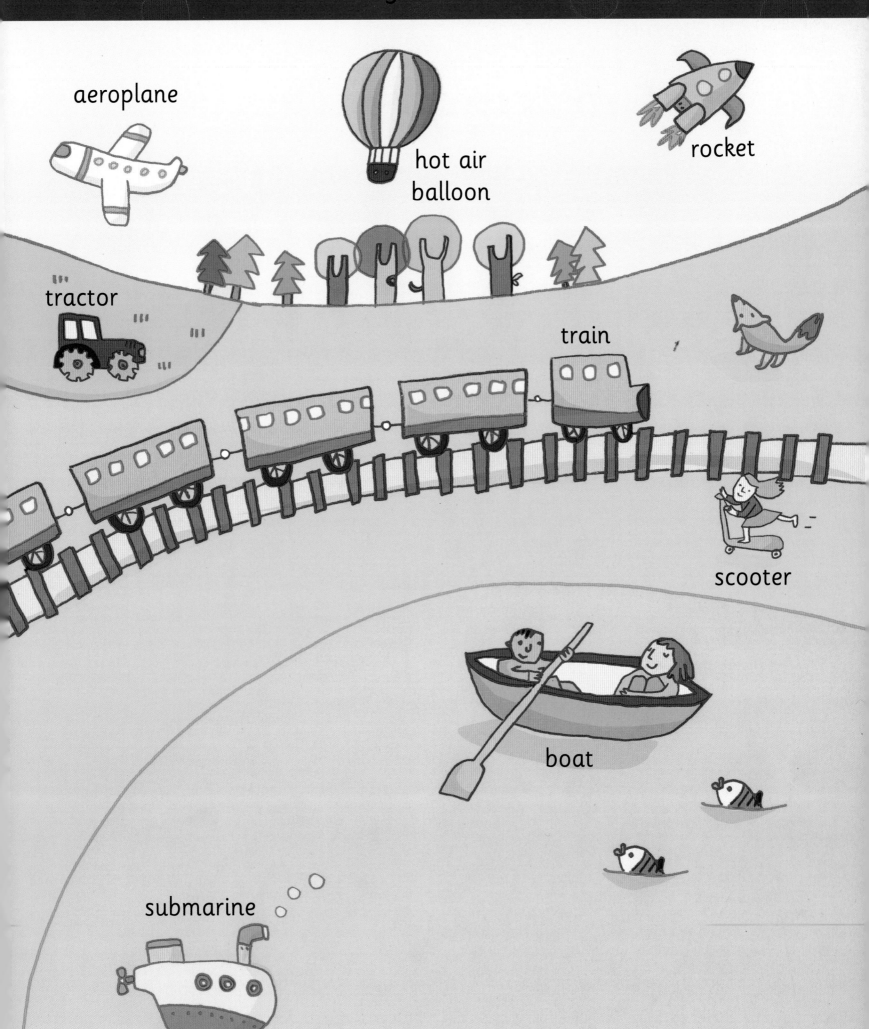

aeroplane

hot air
balloon

rocket

tractor

train

scooter

boat

submarine

Amazing Animals

Point to the pictures and name the different animals you can see.

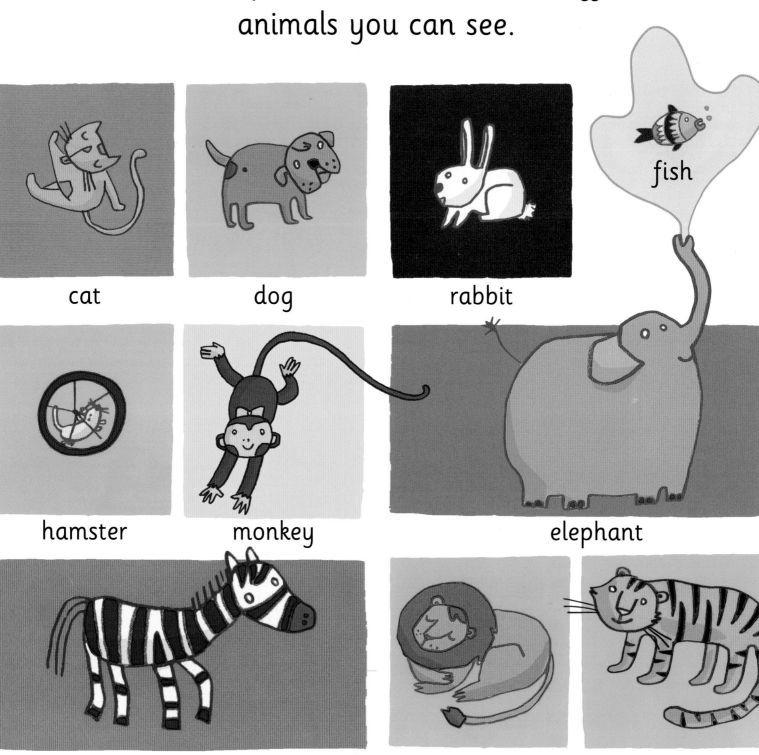

cat

dog

rabbit

fish

hamster

monkey

elephant

zebra

lion

tiger

26

dolphin

penguin

shark

octopus

crab

chicken

duck

sheep

cow

pig

horse

27

Places I Go

There are lots of places to visit when you are out and about.

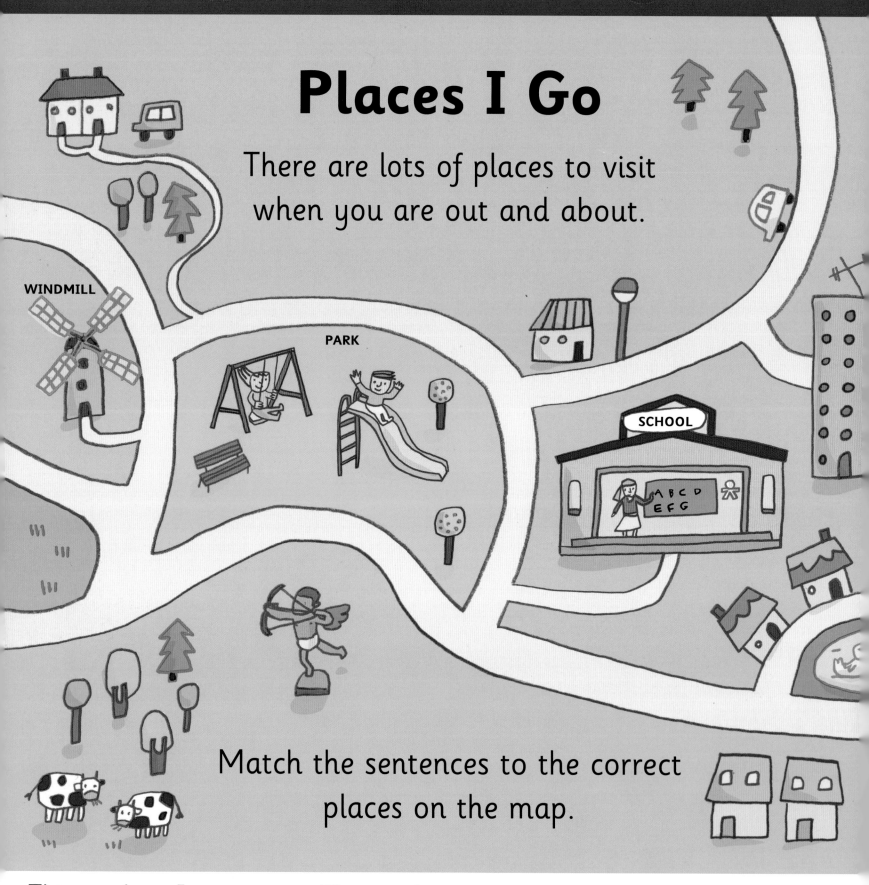

WINDMILL

PARK

SCHOOL

Match the sentences to the correct places on the map.

This is where I go to get my teeth checked.

This is where I go when I don't feel well.

This is where I go to do some shopping.

This is where I go to borrow a book.

This is where I go to learn.

This is where I play on the slide.

Days of the Week

There are seven days in the week.

Monday   **Tuesday**   **Wednesday**   **Thursday**

Friday   **Saturday**   **Sunday**

Point to the pictures and talk about what the children are doing.

Jo is having
a bath.

Ben is getting
dressed.

Kate is eating
her breakfast.

Julia is brushing
her teeth.

John is sleeping
in bed.

Jen is having a
sandwich for lunch.

Jack is
waking up.

Tess is reading
a story.

Ollie is walking
to school.

This little boy has lost ten ice creams.
Can you help him find them all?

Garden Counting

Let's count from eleven to twenty!
Trace the numbers with your finger.

eleven	11
twelve	12
thirteen	13
fourteen	14
fifteen	15
sixteen	16
seventeen	17
eighteen	18
nineteen	19
twenty	20

All About School

The children in your class are
starting school, just like you!

Let's Go to School

At school there will be:

friendly teachers

a coat peg

a desk to sit at

new friends

There will be lots of things to learn:

I will practise
my reading

I will write
stories

I will play on
the computer

I will learn
to swim

The Alphabet Path

At school you will learn your alphabet and begin to read and write.

Follow the alphabet path with your finger.

Aa apple

Bb ball

Cc cat

Dd dog

Hh house

Gg goat

Ff fish

Ee elephant

Mm mouse

Nn net

Ii igloo

Jj jelly

Kk kite

Ll ladybird

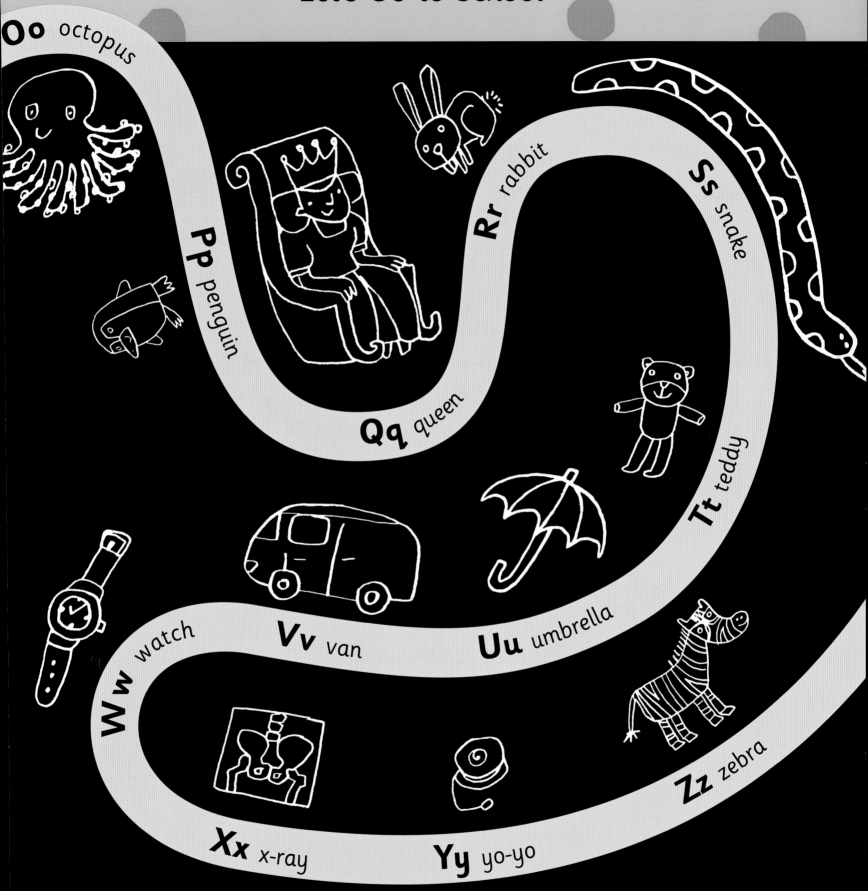

Oo octopus

Pp penguin

Qq queen

Rr rabbit

Ss snake

Tt teddy

Uu umbrella

Vv van

Ww watch

Xx x-ray

Yy yo-yo

Zz zebra

Do you know which letter your name begins with?
Can you write your name?

It's About Time

We use clocks to help us tell the time. The big hand points to the minutes and the little hand points to the hour.

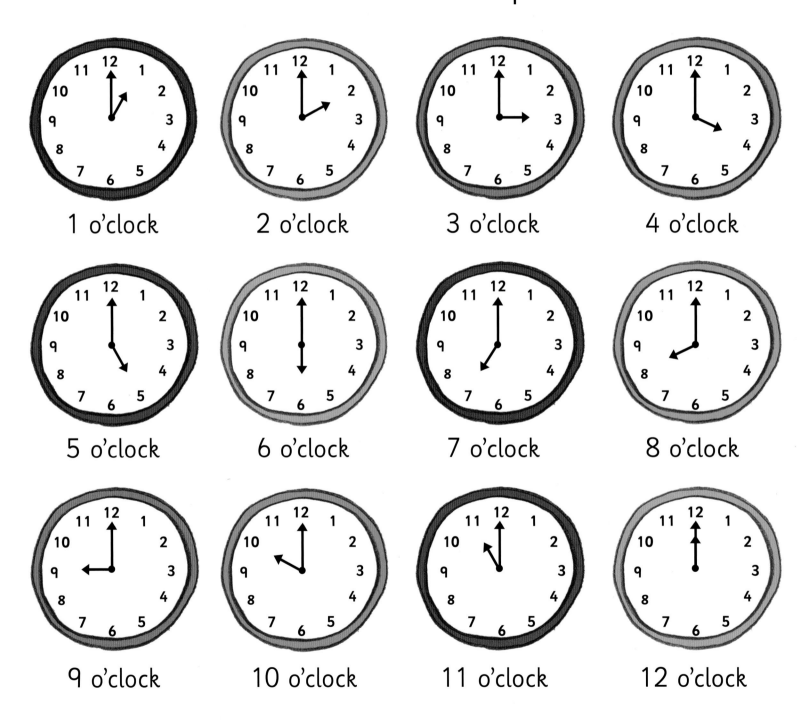

1 o'clock

2 o'clock

3 o'clock

4 o'clock

5 o'clock

6 o'clock

7 o'clock

8 o'clock

9 o'clock

10 o'clock

11 o'clock

12 o'clock

Can you point to 6 o'clock?

Let's Go to School

Look at the pictures. What are the children doing?

At 8 o'clock
I walk to school.

At 11 o'clock
we play in the playground.

At 1 o'clock
we eat our lunch.

At 2 o'clock
it's storytime.

At 3 o'clock it's
time to go home.

Languages of the World

Have a go at saying 'hello' in these different languages!

German

French

Spanish

English

Italian

Mandarin Chinese

Hindi

Polish

New Experiences

Starting school will feel very new!
There is lots to look forward to:

making new friends

learning to read

playing instruments

friendly teachers

drawing and colouring

playing sport

craft activities

lunchtime

storytime

playtime

learning to write

home time

What are you looking forward to about starting school?

Now I'm Ready for School

I get up.

I eat my breakfast.

I brush my teeth.

I get dressed.

I pack my lunch.

I collect my book bag.

I put on my coat.

I walk to school.

I say 'hello' to my friends.

I go into my classroom.

I'm Ready... for Phonics!

Say the Sounds

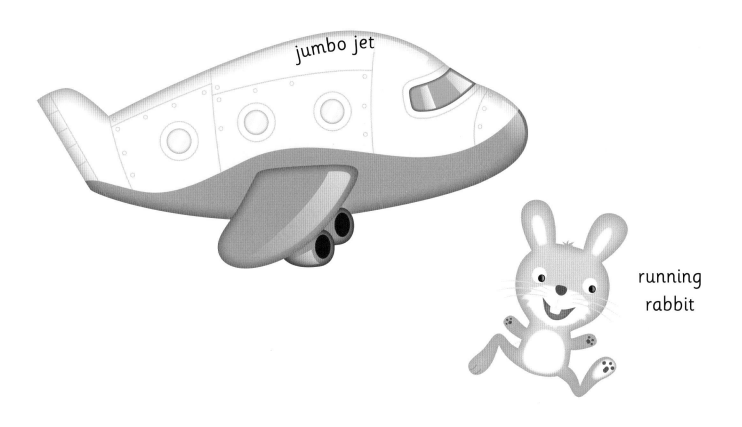

jumbo jet

running rabbit

Illustrated by Ian Cunliffe

Say the Sounds

This is ideal for children who are starting out on their reading journey. It focuses on the sound at the beginning of each word – teachers call this the initial letter sound. Learning these sounds is the first building block to successful reading.

Recognizing these initial letter sounds is a vital step in your child's synthetic phonics learning.

For more advice about phonics and for further activities visit **www.ladybird.com**

What is the difference between A and a?

A is a letter name. Letter names are the letters of the alphabet.

a is a letter sound. Letter sounds are the sounds the letters make.

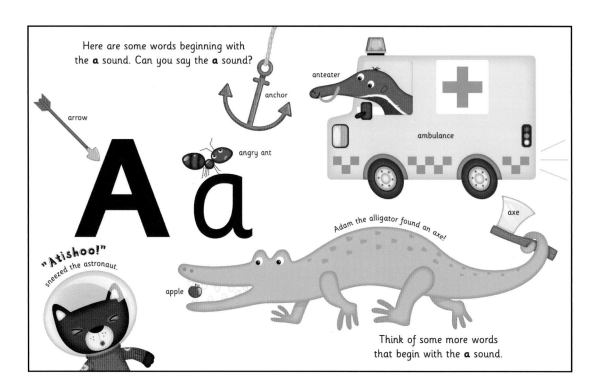

Here are some words beginning with the **a** sound. Can you say the **a** sound?

arrow

anchor

anteater

angry ant

ambulance

axe

Adam the alligator found an axe!

"Atishoo!" sneezed the astronaut.

apple

Think of some more words that begin with the **a** sound.

Tips on how to use these pages with your child:

Read the simple question to your child and say the sound together.

Have fun pointing to the different pictures on the page. Can your child name them all?

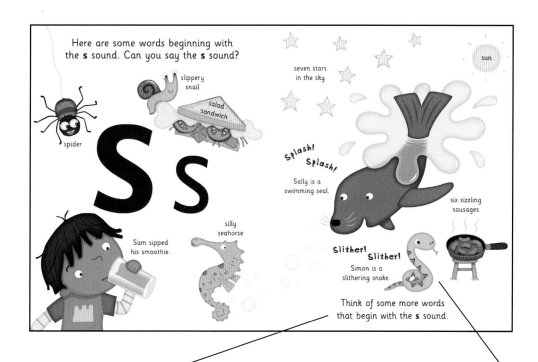

Using the instructions and questions, encourage your child to have fun with the initial letter sound he can hear.

Make up a story together using the objects and characters on the page. Remember to have fun and don't be afraid of being silly!

Is Simon a dancing snake? No, Simon is a slithering snake. Simon slithers towards six sizzling sausages.

Here are some words beginning with the **a** sound. Can you say the **a** sound?

anchor

arrow

angry ant

A a

"Atishoo!" sneezed the astronaut.

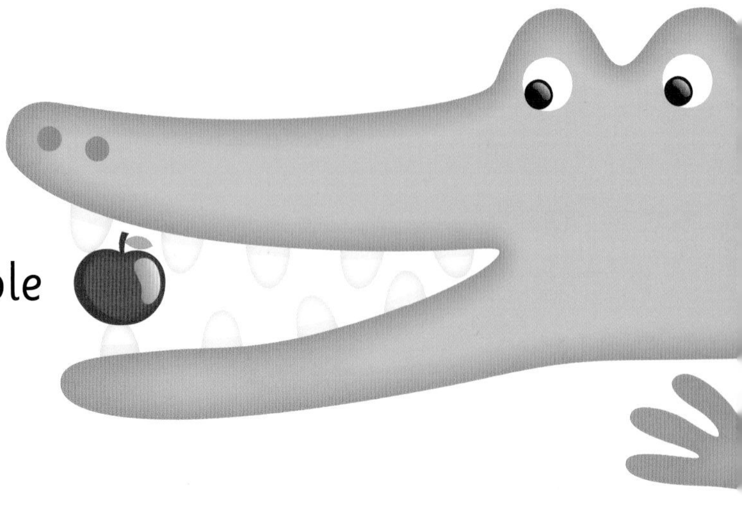

apple

anteater

ambulance

axe

Adam the alligator found an axe!

Think of some more words
that begin with the **a** sound.

Here are some words beginning with the **b** sound.
Can you say the **b** sound?

Brring! Brring!

Ben's brand new bike

bouncy ball

B b

blue bat

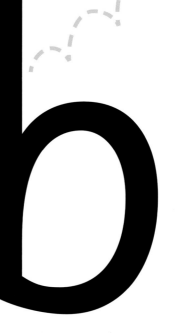

bouncy ball

Beep! Beep!

Buzz! Buzz!

busy bee

Bob the bat has a boat.

Count all the animals beginning
with **b** on the page.

Here are some words beginning with the **c** sound.
Can you say the **c** sound?

Clip! Clop!

cup

cap

camel

C c

"Crumbs!"
said Callum
the clumsy clown.

cake

crooked car

Crash!

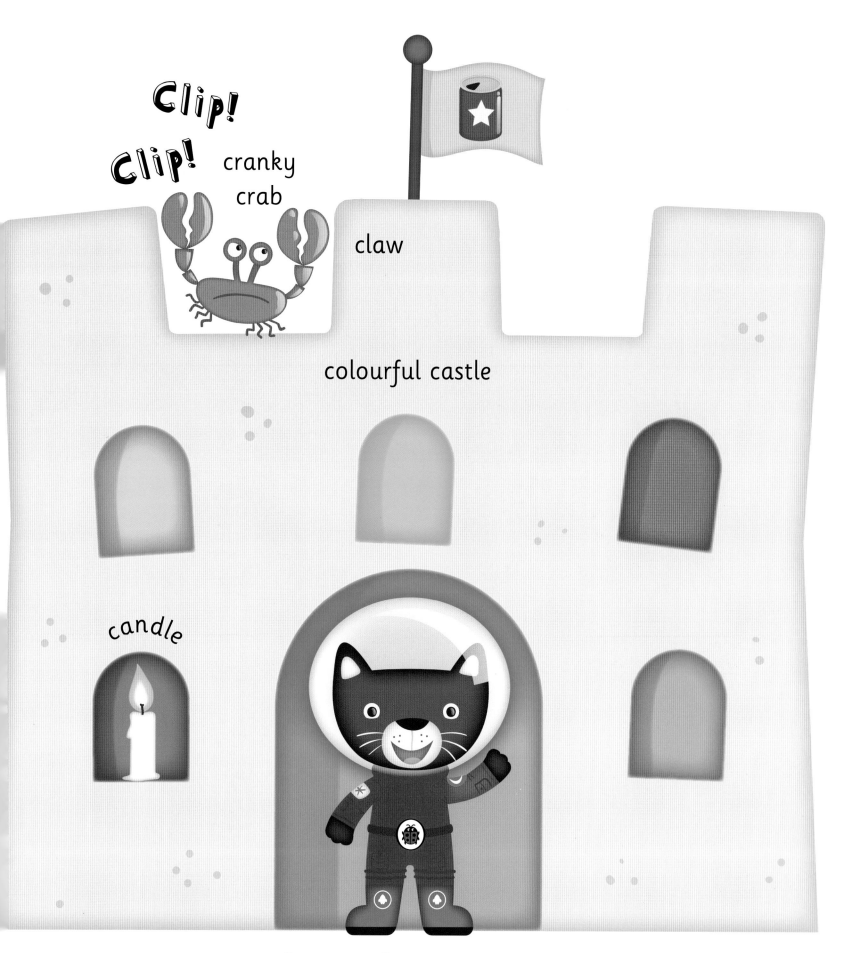

Clip! Clip! cranky crab

claw

colourful castle

candle

Captain Comet is a cat.

As you say the words,
try to make the **c** sound stand out.

Here are some words beginning with the **d** sound. Can you say the **d** sound?

delighted dinosaur

diving dolphin

dotty dice

duck

D d

Dan the donkey throws a dart.

Doink!

dartboard

66

Ding!
Dong!

Daisy the doll rings
the doorbell.

door

Dad has a
dusty drill.

dancing
dog

dangerous
dragon

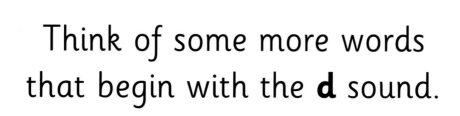

Think of some more words
that begin with the **d** sound.

Here are some words beginning with the **e** sound. Can you say the **e** sound?

E e

Ed is an energetic elephant

emerald

emperor

empty envelope

Ellie the elf
is excited.

elegant
egg

As you say the words,
try to make the **e** sound stand out.

Here are some words beginning with the **f** sound. Can you say the **f** sound?

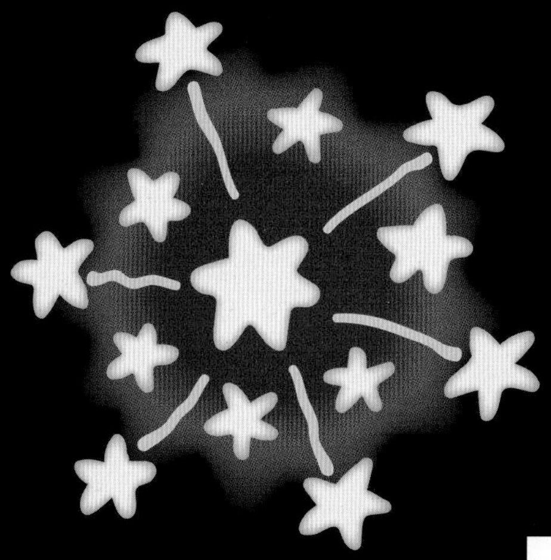

Fizz! Fizz!

four fabulous fireworks

F f

fork

fence

Fred the farmer chased the fox with a fork.

fox

Flutter!
Flutter!

fancy butterfly

feathers

funny
flamingo

As you say the words,
try to make the **f** sound stand out.

Here are some words beginning with the **g** sound.
Can you say the **g** sound?

greedy
grey goat

"Grr! Grr!"
grumbled the
grumpy gorilla.

grape

G g

golden goose

Gita gave
Grace a gift.

green grass

"Growl! Growl!" grizzled Gordon the grizzly bear.

"Gurgle! Gurgle!" giggled the baby girl.

guitar

Count all the animals beginning with **g** on the page.

Here are some words beginning with the **h** sound. Can you say the **h** sound?

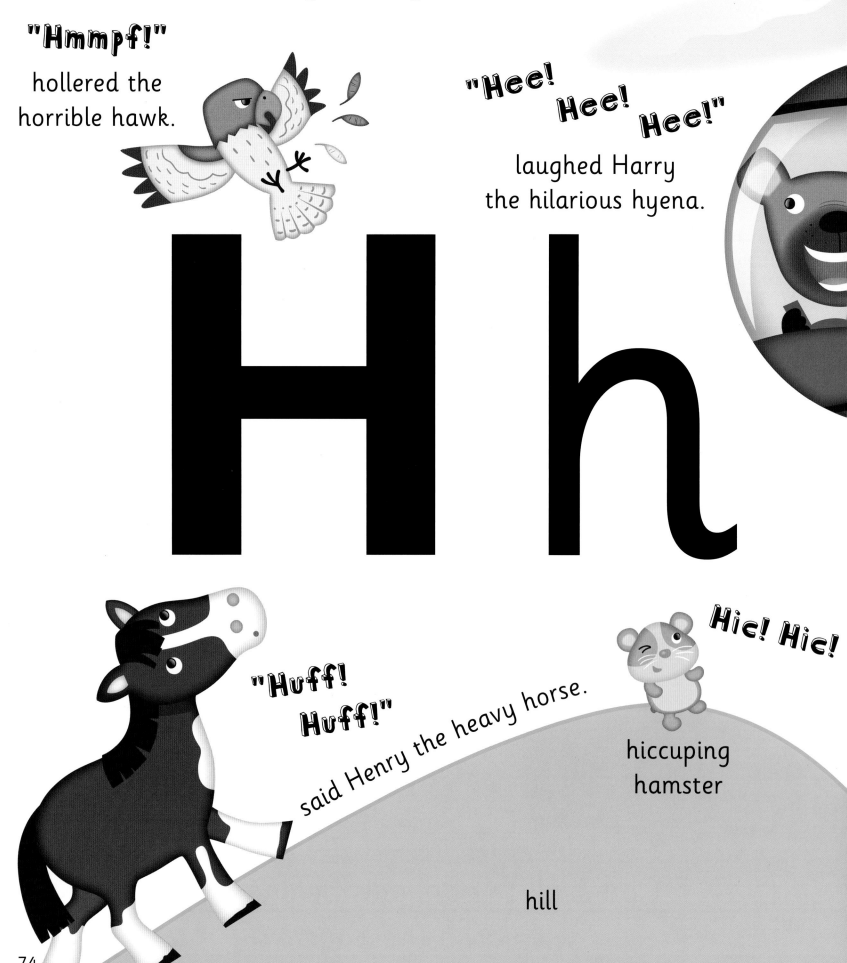

"Hmmpf!"
hollered the horrible hawk.

"Hee! Hee! Hee!"
laughed Harry the hilarious hyena.

H h

"Huff! Huff!"
said Henry the heavy horse.

Hic! Hic!
hiccuping hamster

hill

74

helicopter

henhouse

happy
hen

Hester is a
hairy hippo.

Think of some more words
that begin with the **h** sound.

Here are some words beginning with the **i** sound.
Can you say the **i** sound?

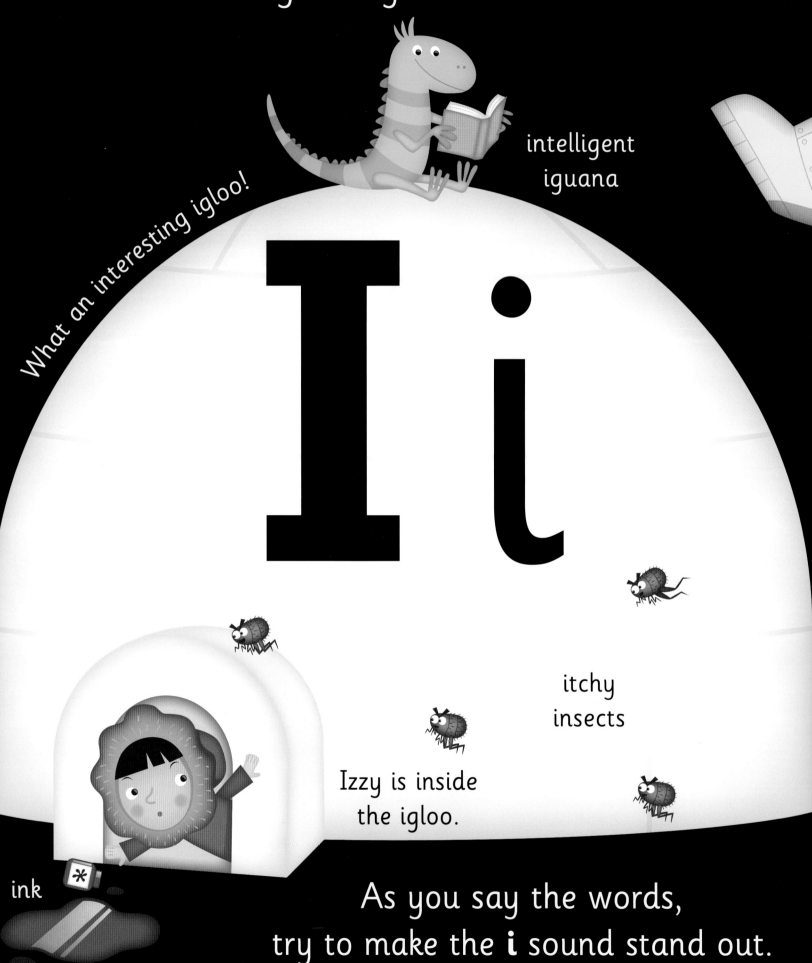

intelligent
iguana

What an interesting igloo!

Ii

itchy
insects

Izzy is inside
the igloo.

ink

As you say the words,
try to make the **i** sound stand out.

Here are some words beginning with the **j** sound.
Can you say the **j** sound?

jumbo jet

John is a
jolly juggler.

J j

jiggling jellyfish

Jump!
Jump!

jumping
Jack-in-the-box

Think of some more words
that begin with the **j** sound.

Here are some words beginning with the **k** sound.
Can you say the **k** sound?

kite

kind king

koala

kicking
kangaroo

keys

As you say the words,
try to make the **k** sound stand out.

Here are some words beginning with the l sound. Can you say the l sound?

long lobster

little ladybird

"La, la, la!" sang the lively lizard.

log

L l

Larry is a large lazy lion.

Lick! Lick!

lovely lollipop

Think of some more words that begin with the l sound.

Here are some words beginning with the **m** sound. Can you say the **m** sound?

misty moon

marvellous magician

magic mirror

80

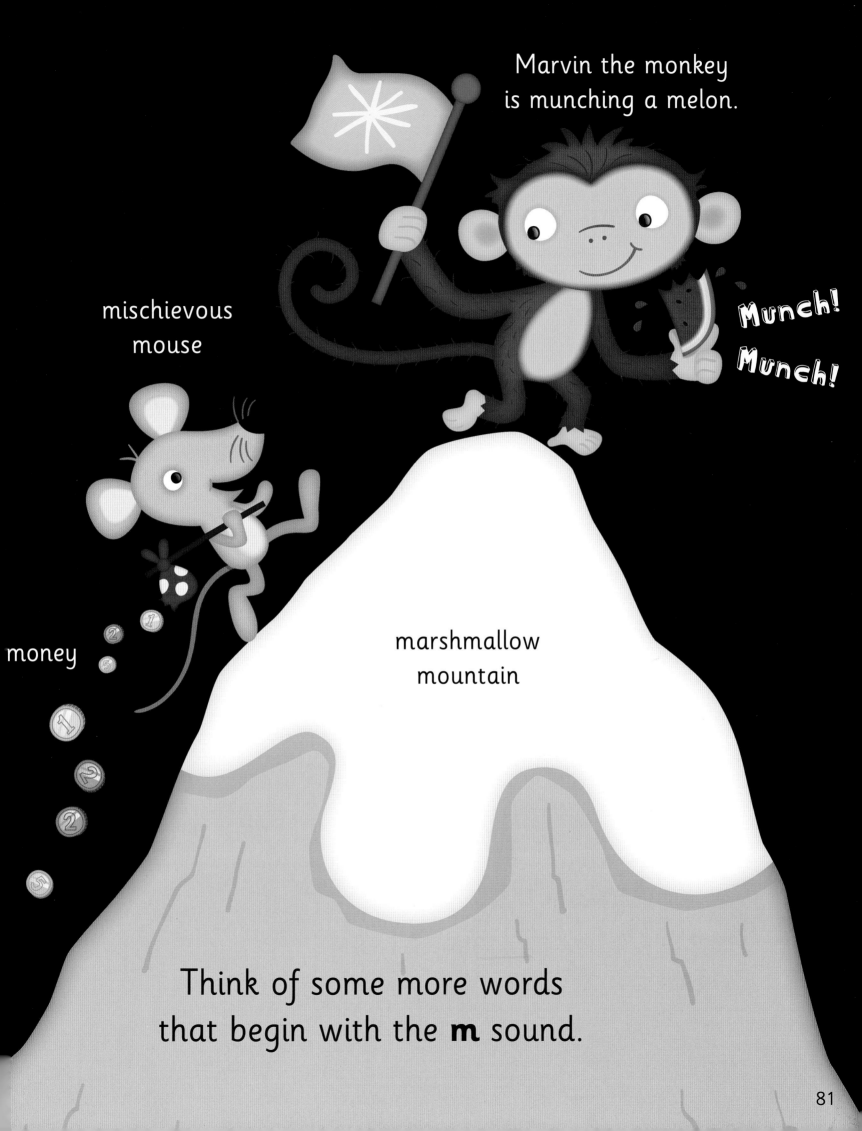

Marvin the monkey
is munching a melon.

mischievous
mouse

Munch!
Munch!

money

marshmallow
mountain

Think of some more words
that begin with the **m** sound.

Here are some words beginning with the **n** sound. Can you say the **n** sound?

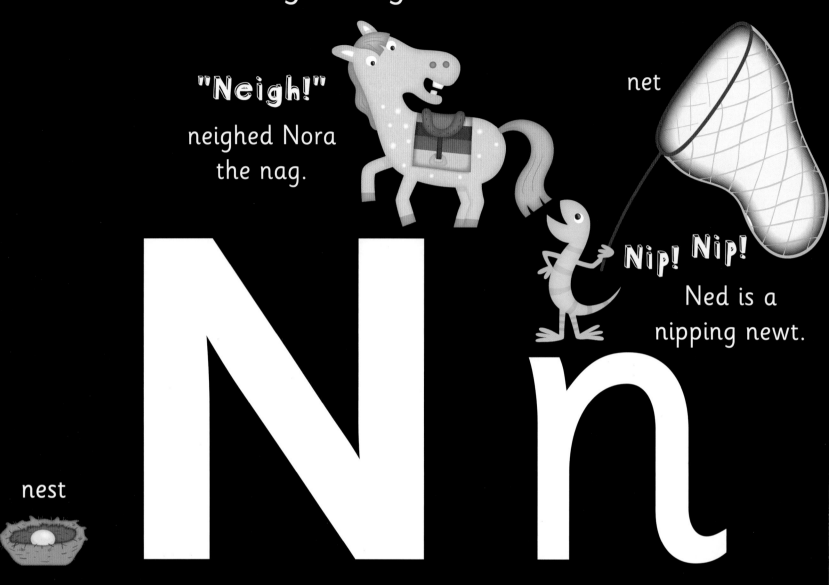

"Neigh!"

neighed Nora the nag.

net

Nip! Nip!

Ned is a nipping newt.

nest

N n

nine nosy neighbours

As you say the words,
try to make the **n** sound stand out.

Here are some words beginning with the **o** sound.
Can you say the **o** sound?

octopus

ostrich

O o

ox

oranges

oblong

odd otter

Count all the animals beginning
with **o** on the page.

Here are some words beginning with the **p** sound.
Can you say the **p** sound?

"Puff! Puff!"
said Polly the puffing panda.

prickly pineapple

Percy is a pink pig.

purple parrot

perch

Pitter! Patter!

prancing polar bear

POP!

POP!

POP!

popping peas

pretty penguin

As you say the words,
try to make the **p** sound stand out.

Here are some words beginning with the **q** sound.
Can you say the **q** sound?

quilt

quiet queen

quarter

"Quack!
Quack!"
quacked the
ducks.

As you say the words,
try to make the **q** sound stand out.

Here are some words beginning with the **r** sound.
Can you say the **r** sound?

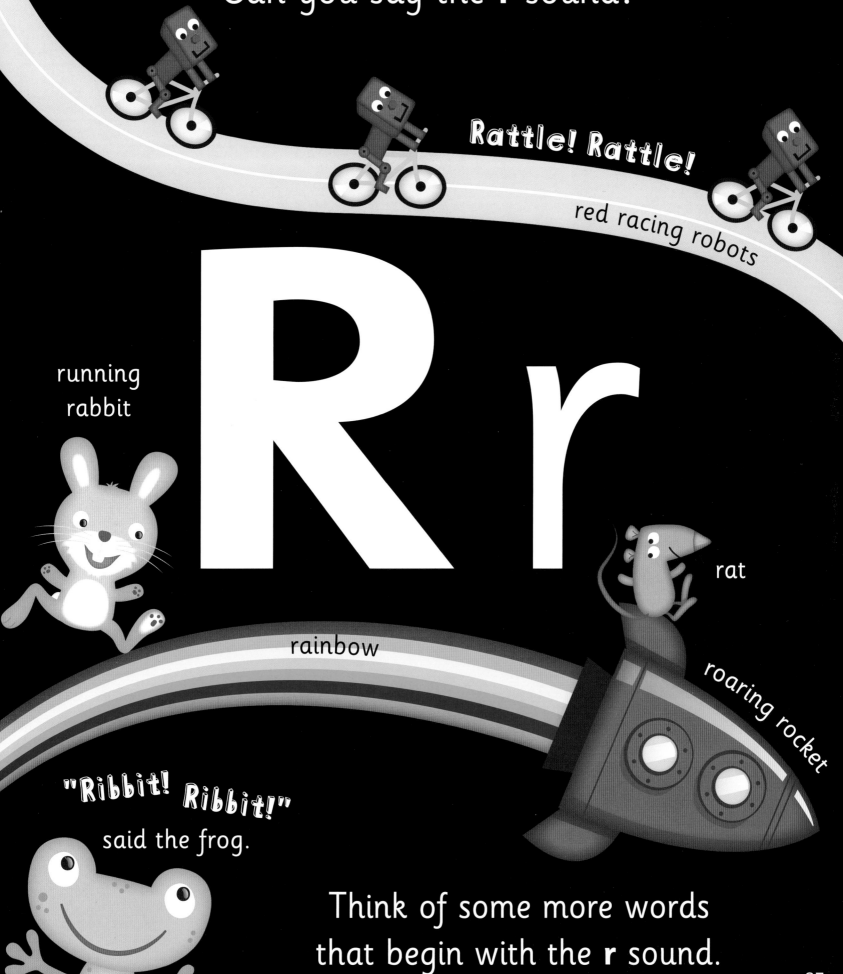

Rattle! Rattle!

red racing robots

running
rabbit

Rr

rat

rainbow

roaring rocket

"Ribbit! Ribbit!"
said the frog.

Think of some more words
that begin with the **r** sound.

Here are some words beginning with the **s** sound. Can you say the **s** sound?

slippery
snail

salad
sandwich

spider

S s

silly
seahorse

Sam sipped
his smoothie.

88

sun

seven stars
in the sky

Splash!

Splash!

Sally is a
swimming seal.

six sizzling
sausages

Slither!

Slither!

Simon is a
slithering snake.

Think of some more words
that begin with the **s** sound.

Here are some words beginning with the **t** sound.
Can you say the **t** sound?

Tickle! Tickle!

terrific tortoise

turquoise teddy

trifle

tomatoes

ten tiny tractors

"Tut! Tut!"
tutted Tina
the tiger.

"Tweet! Tweet!"
twittered two turtle doves.

tea

teapot

toast

tail

table

Tick! Tock!

ticking clock

toad

As you say the words,
try to make the **t** sound stand out.

Here are some words beginning with the **u** sound.
Can you say the **u** sound?

upside-down umbrella

Up! Up! Up!

"Uh-oh!"
said Uncle.

Uncle's ugly underwear

As you say the words,
try to make the **u** sound stand out.

Here are some words beginning with the **v** sound.
Can you say the **v** sound?

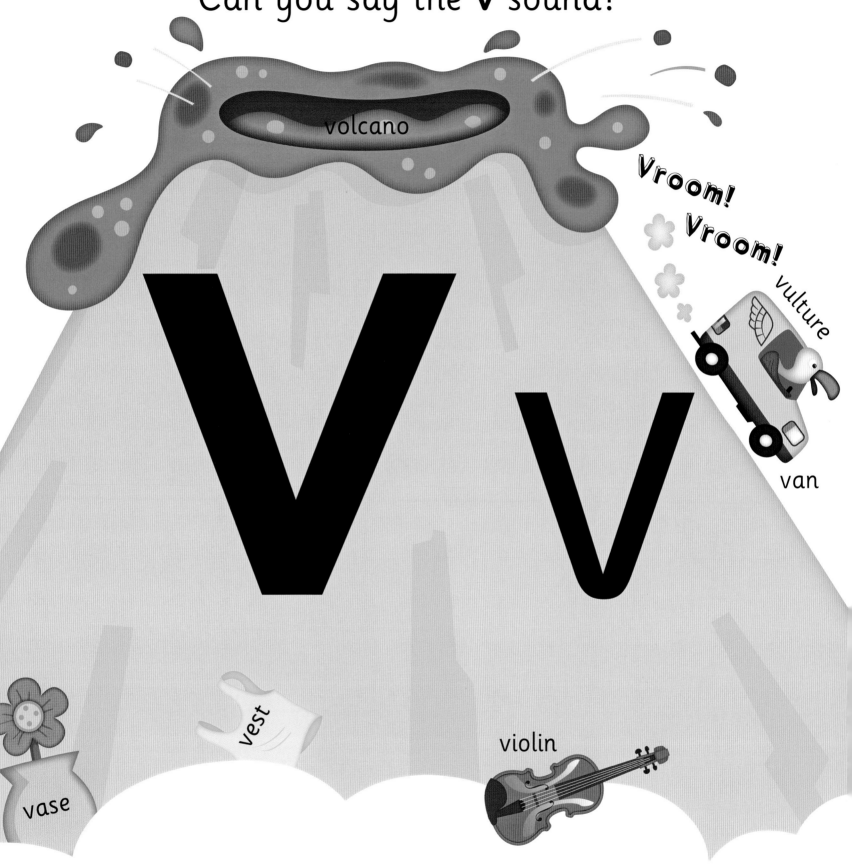

volcano

Vroom! Vroom!

vulture

van

vest

violin

vase

Think of some more words
that begin with the **v** sound.

Here are some words beginning with the **w** sound.
Can you say the **w** sound?

wicked witch

"Woo! Woo!"

wailed Wendy the wolf.

Walter is a wet walrus.

wiggly worm

Count all the animals beginning with **w** on the page.

Here are some words beginning with **x**.

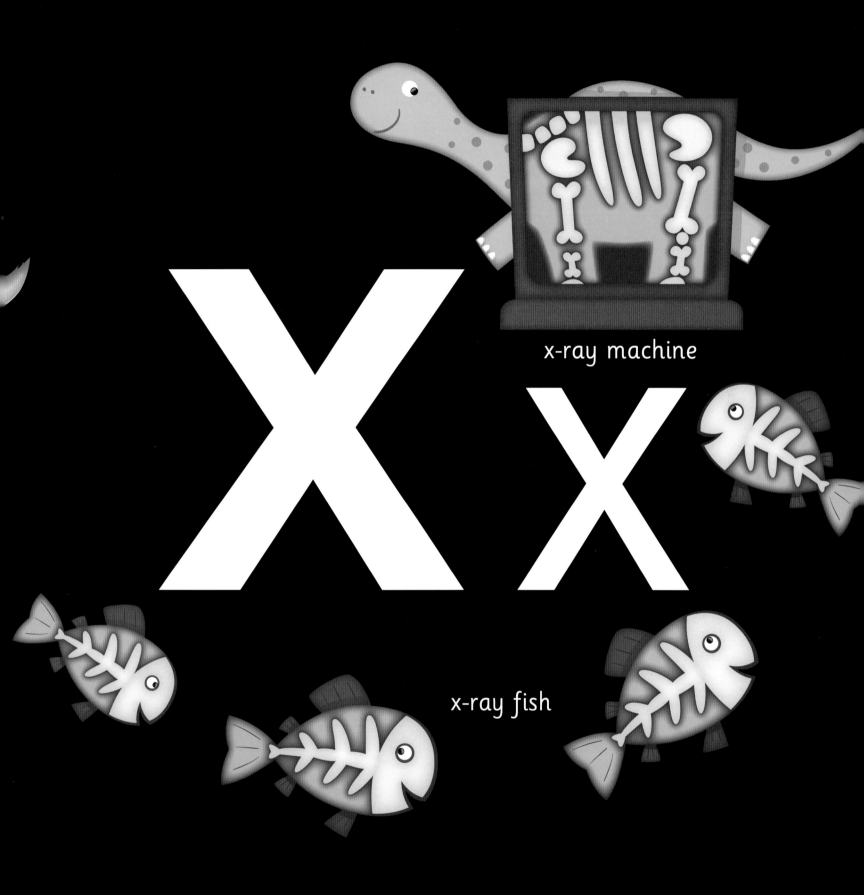

x-ray machine

x-ray fish

When you say the words, try to make
the **x** at the front of the word stand out.

Here are some words beginning with the **y** sound. Can you say the **y** sound?

yawning
yak

Yawn!
Yawn!

Yy

"yes!"
yelled Yan.

yummy
yoghurt

yellow yo-yo

Think of some more words
that begin with the **y** sound.

Here are some words beginning with the **z** sound.
Can you say the **z** sound?

Zoom! Zoom!

zip

Zzz! Zzz!

Zelda the sleepy zebra.

zombie

zig-zagging zoo car

zoo keeper

As you say the words,
try to make the **z** sound stand out.

I'm Ready... to Sing!

Illustrated by Sonia Esplugas

Old MacDonald had a Farm

Old MacDonald had a farm, E I E I O,
And on that farm he had a cow, E I E I O.
With a moo-moo here and a moo-moo there,
Here a moo, there a moo, everywhere a moo-moo.
Old MacDonald had a farm, E I E I O.

Old MacDonald had a farm, E I E I O,
And on that farm he had a sheep, E I E I O.
With a baa-baa here and a baa-baa there,
Here a baa, there a baa, everywhere a baa-baa.
Old MacDonald had a farm, E I E I O.

Old MacDonald had a farm, E I E I O,
And on that farm he had a pig, E I E I O.
With an oink-oink here and an oink-oink there,
Here an oink, there an oink, everywhere an oink-oink.
Old MacDonald had a farm, E I E I O.

Old MacDonald had a farm, E I E I O,
And on his farm he had a duck, E I E I O.
With a quack-quack here and a quack-quack there,
Here a quack, there a quack, everywhere a quack-quack.
Old MacDonald had a farm, E I E I O.

Old MacDonald had a farm, E I E I O,
And on that farm he had a horse, E I E I O.
With a neigh-neigh here and a neigh-neigh there,
Here a neigh, there a neigh, everywhere a neigh-neigh.
Old MacDonald had a farm, E I E I O.

The House that Jack Built

This is the house that Jack built!
This is the malt that lay in the house that Jack built.
This is the rat that ate the malt,
That lay in the house that Jack built.

This is the cat that killed the rat,
That ate the malt that lay in the house that Jack built.
This is the dog that worried the cat,
That killed the rat that ate the malt,
That lay in the house that Jack built.

This is the cow with the crumpled horn,
That tossed the dog that worried the cat,
That killed the rat that ate the malt,
That lay in the house that Jack built.

This is the maiden all forlorn,
That milked the cow with the crumpled horn,
That tossed the dog that worried the cat,
That killed the rat that ate the malt,
That lay in the house that Jack built.

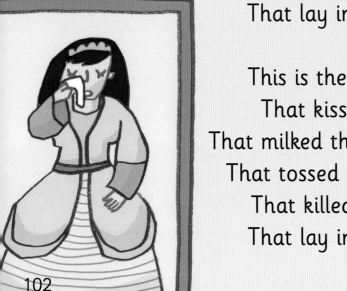

This is the man all tattered and torn,
That kissed the maiden all forlorn,
That milked the cow with the crumpled horn,
That tossed the dog that worried the cat,
That killed the rat that ate the malt,
That lay in the house that Jack built.

This is the priest all shaven and shorn,
That married the man all tattered and torn,
That kissed the maiden all forlorn,
That milked the cow with the crumpled horn,
That tossed the dog that worried the cat,
That killed the rat that ate the malt,
That lay in the house that Jack built.

This is the cock that crowed in the morn,
That woke the priest all shaven and shorn,
That married the man all tattered and torn,
That kissed the maiden all forlorn,
That milked the cow with the crumpled horn,
That tossed the dog that worried the cat,
That killed the rat that ate the malt,
That lay in the house that Jack built.

This is the farmer sowing his corn,
That kept the cock that crowed in the morn,
That woke the priest all shaven and shorn,
That married the man all tattered and torn,
That kissed the maiden all forlorn,
That milked the cow with the crumpled horn,
That tossed the dog that worried the cat,
That killed the rat that ate the malt,
That lay in the house that Jack built!

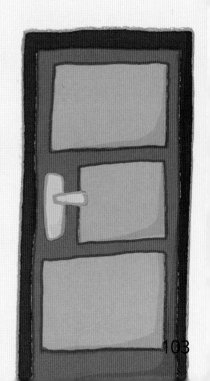

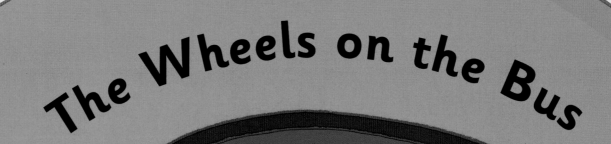

The Wheels on the Bus

The wheels on the bus go round and round,
Round and round, round and round,
The wheels on the bus go round and round,
All day long.

The wipers on the bus go swish-swish-swish,
Swish-swish-swish, swish-swish-swish,
The wipers on the bus go swish-swish-swish,
All day long.

The horn on the bus goes beep-beep-beep,
Beep-beep-beep, beep-beep-beep,
The horn on the bus goes beep beep beep,
All day long.

The children on the bus go up and down,
Up and down, up and down,
The children on the bus go up and down,
All day long.

The babies on the bus go wah-wah-wah,
Wah-wah-wah, wah-wah-wah,
The babies on the bus go wah-wah-wah,
All day long.

The mums on the bus go ssh-ssh-ssh,
Ssh-ssh-ssh, ssh-ssh-ssh,
The mums on the bus go ssh-ssh-ssh,
All day long.

London Bridge is Falling Down

London Bridge is falling down,
Falling down, falling down,
London Bridge is falling down,
My fair lady.

Row, Row, Row Your Boat

Row, row, row your boat,
Gently down the stream,
Merrily, merrily, merrily, merrily,
Life is but a dream.

Row, row, row your boat,
Gently down the stream,
If you see a crocodile,
Don't forget to scream –

Arghh!

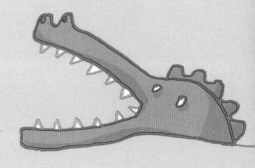

There Was an Old Lady Who Swallowed a Fly

There was an old lady who swallowed a fly;
I don't know why she swallowed a fly —
Perhaps she'll die!

There was an old lady who swallowed a spider,
That wriggled and wiggled and jiggled inside her;
She swallowed the spider to catch the fly;
I don't know why she swallowed a fly —
Perhaps she'll die!

There was an old lady who swallowed a bird,
How absurd to swallow a bird!
She swallowed the bird to catch the spider,
She swallowed the spider to catch the fly;
I don't know why she swallowed a fly —
Perhaps she'll die!

There was an old lady who swallowed a cat,
Fancy that to swallow a cat!
She swallowed the cat to catch the bird,
She swallowed the bird to catch the spider,
She swallowed the spider to catch the fly;
I don't know why she swallowed a fly —
Perhaps she'll die!

There was an old lady who swallowed a dog,
What a hog, to swallow a dog!
She swallowed the dog to catch the cat,
She swallowed the cat to catch the bird,
She swallowed the bird to catch the spider,
She swallowed the spider to catch the fly;
I don't know why she swallowed a fly –
Perhaps she'll die!

There was an old lady who swallowed a cow,
I don't know how she swallowed a cow!
She swallowed the cow to catch the dog,
She swallowed the dog to catch the cat,
She swallowed the cat to catch the bird,
She swallowed the bird to catch the spider,
She swallowed the spider to catch the fly;
I don't know why she swallowed a fly –
Perhaps she'll die!

There was an old lady who swallowed a horse...
She's dead, of course!

Ten in the Bed

There were ten in the bed and the little one said,
"Roll over! Roll over!"
So they all rolled over and one fell out.

There were nine in the bed and the little one said,
"Roll over! Roll over!"
So they all rolled over and one fell out.

There were eight in the bed and the little one said,
"Roll over! Roll over!"
So they all rolled over and one fell out.

There were seven in the bed and the little one said,
"Roll over! Roll over!"
So they all rolled over and one fell out.

There were six in the bed and the little one said,
"Roll over! Roll over!"
So they all rolled over and one fell out.

There were five in the bed and the little one said,
"Roll over! Roll over!"
So they all rolled over and one fell out.

There were four in the bed and the little one said,
"Roll over! Roll over!"
So they all rolled over and one fell out.

There were three in the bed and the little one said,
"Roll over! Roll over!"
So they all rolled over and one fell out.

There were two in the bed and the little one said,
"Roll over! Roll over!"
So they all rolled over and one fell out.

There was one in the bed and the little one said,
"Good night!"

If You're Happy and You Know it

If you're happy and you know it clap your hands.
If you're happy and you know it clap your hands.
If you're happy and you know it and you really want to show it,
If you're happy and you know it clap your hands.

If you're happy and you know it stomp your feet.
If you're happy and you know it stomp your feet.
If you're happy and you know it and you really want to show it,
If you're happy and you know it stomp your feet.

If you're happy and you know it shout, "Hooray!"
If you're happy and you know it shout, "Hooray!"
If you're happy and you know it and you really want to show it,
If you're happy and you know it shout, "Hooray!"

If you're happy and you know it do all three.
If you're happy and you know it do all three.
If you're happy and you know it and you really want to show it,
If you're happy and you know it do all three!

Wind the Bobbin Up

Wind the bobbin up,
Wind the bobbin up.
Pull, pull,
Clap, clap, clap.
Wind it back again,
Wind it back again.
Pull, pull,
Clap, clap, clap.

Point to the ceiling,
Point to the floor,
Point to the window,
Point to the door.
Clap your hands together,
One, two, three.
Put your hands
Upon your knee.

Five Little Speckled Frogs

Five little speckled frogs,
Sat on a speckled log,
Eating some most delicious bugs
yum, yum!

One jumped into the pool,
Where it was nice and cool,
Then there were four speckled frogs
glug, glug!

Four little speckled frogs,
Sat on a speckled log,
Eating some most delicious bugs
yum, yum!

One jumped into the pool,
Where it was nice and cool,
Then there were three speckled frogs
glug, glug!

Three little speckled frogs,
Sat on a speckled log,
Eating some most delicious bugs
yum, yum!

One jumped into the pool,
Where it was nice and cool,
Then there were two speckled frogs
glug, glug!

Two little speckled frogs,
Sat on a speckled log,
Eating some most delicious bugs
yum, yum!

One jumped into the pool,
Where it was nice and cool,
Then there was one speckled frog
glug, glug!

One little speckled frog,
Sat on a speckled log,
Eating some most delicious bugs
yum, yum!

He jumped into the pool,
Where it was nice and cool,

Then there were **no** speckled frogs.

One Man Went to Mow

One man went to mow, went to mow a meadow.
One man and his dog,
Woof!
Went to mow a meadow.

Two men went to mow, went to mow a meadow,
Two men, one man and his dog,
Woof!
Went to mow a meadow.

Three men went to mow, went to mow a meadow,
Three men, two men, one man and his dog,
Woof!
Went to mow a meadow.

Four men went to mow, went to mow a meadow,
Four men, three men, two men, one man and his dog,
Woof!
Went to mow a meadow.

Five men went to mow, went to mow a meadow,
Five men, four men, three men, two men, one man and his dog,
Woof!
Went to mow a meadow.

This Old Man

This old man, he played one,
He played knick-knack on my thumb;
With a knick-knack paddy whack give a dog a bone,
This old man came rolling home.

This old man, he played two,
He played knick-knack on my shoe;
With a knick-knack paddy whack give a dog a bone,
This old man came rolling home.

This old man, he played three,
He played knick-knack on my knee;
With a knick-knack paddy whack give a dog a bone,
This old man came rolling home.

This old man, he played four,
He played knick-knack on the floor;
With a knick-knack paddy whack give a dog a bone,
This old man came rolling home.

This old man, he played five,
He played knick-knack on my hive;
With a knick-knack paddy whack give a dog a bone,
This old man came rolling home.

This old man, he played six,
He played knick-knack on some sticks;
With a knick-knack paddy whack give a dog a bone,
This old man came rolling home.

This old man, he played seven,
He played knick-knack up in heaven;
With a knick-knack paddy whack give a dog a bone,
This old man came rolling home.

This old man, he played eight,
He played knick-knack at my gate;
With a knick-knack paddy whack give a dog a bone,
This old man came rolling home.

This old man, he played nine,
He played knick-knack on my spine;
With a knick-knack paddy whack give a dog a bone,
This old man came rolling home.

This old man, he played ten,
He played knick-knack once again;
With a knick-knack paddy whack give a dog a bone,
This old man came rolling home.

Five Little Monkeys

Five little monkeys jumping on the bed,
One fell off and bumped his head.
Mummy called the doctor and the doctor said,
"No more monkeys jumping on the bed!"

Four little monkeys jumping on the bed,
One fell off and bumped her head.
Mummy called the doctor and the doctor said,
"No more monkeys jumping on the bed!"

Three little monkeys jumping on the bed,
One fell off and bumped his head.
Mummy called the doctor and the doctor said,
"No more monkeys jumping on the bed!"

Two little monkeys jumping on the bed,
One fell off and bumped her head.
Mummy called the doctor and the doctor said,
"No more monkeys jumping on the bed!"

One little monkey jumping on the bed,
He fell off and bumped his head.
Mummy called the doctor and the doctor said,
"Put those monkeys straight to bed!"

Incy Wincy Spider

Incy Wincy spider climbed up the waterspout,
Down came the rain and washed the spider out,
Out came the sun and dried up all the rain,
So Incy Wincy spider climbed up the spout again.

Down in the Jungle

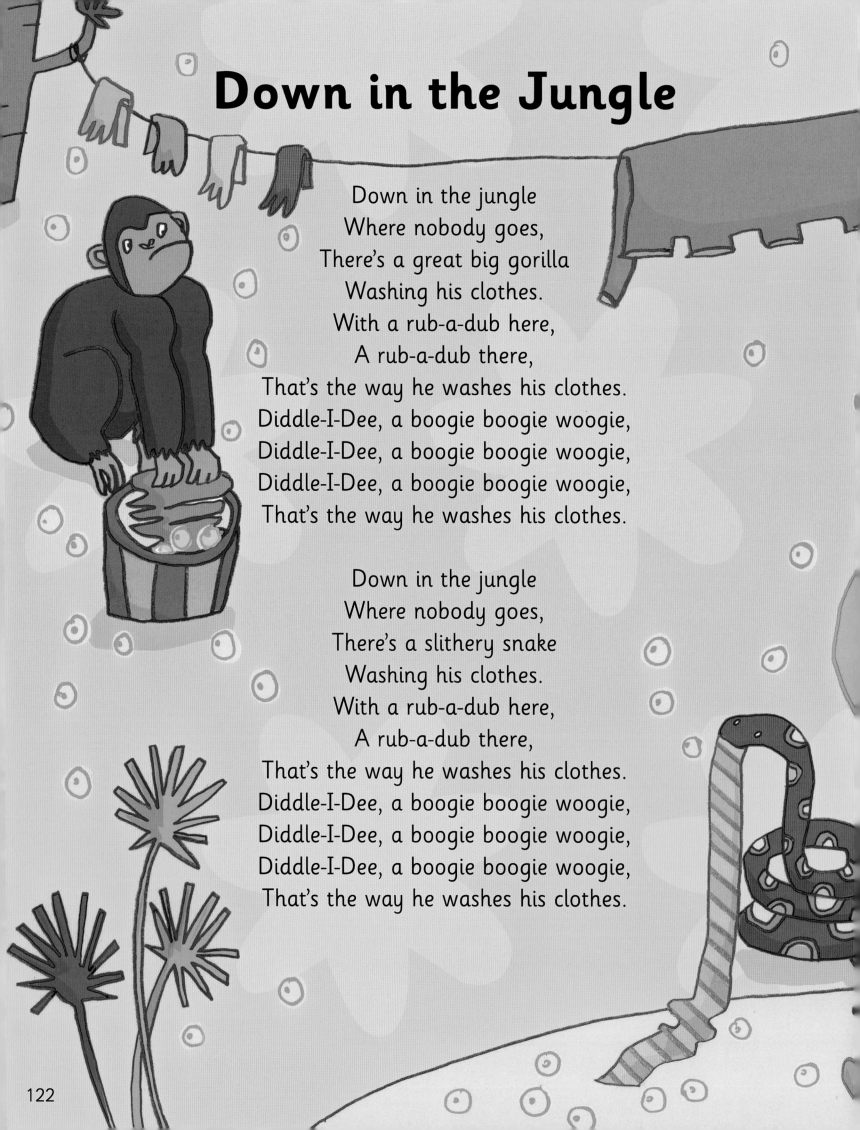

Down in the jungle
Where nobody goes,
There's a great big gorilla
Washing his clothes.
With a rub-a-dub here,
A rub-a-dub there,
That's the way he washes his clothes.
Diddle-I-Dee, a boogie boogie woogie,
Diddle-I-Dee, a boogie boogie woogie,
Diddle-I-Dee, a boogie boogie woogie,
That's the way he washes his clothes.

Down in the jungle
Where nobody goes,
There's a slithery snake
Washing his clothes.
With a rub-a-dub here,
A rub-a-dub there,
That's the way he washes his clothes.
Diddle-I-Dee, a boogie boogie woogie,
Diddle-I-Dee, a boogie boogie woogie,
Diddle-I-Dee, a boogie boogie woogie,
That's the way he washes his clothes.

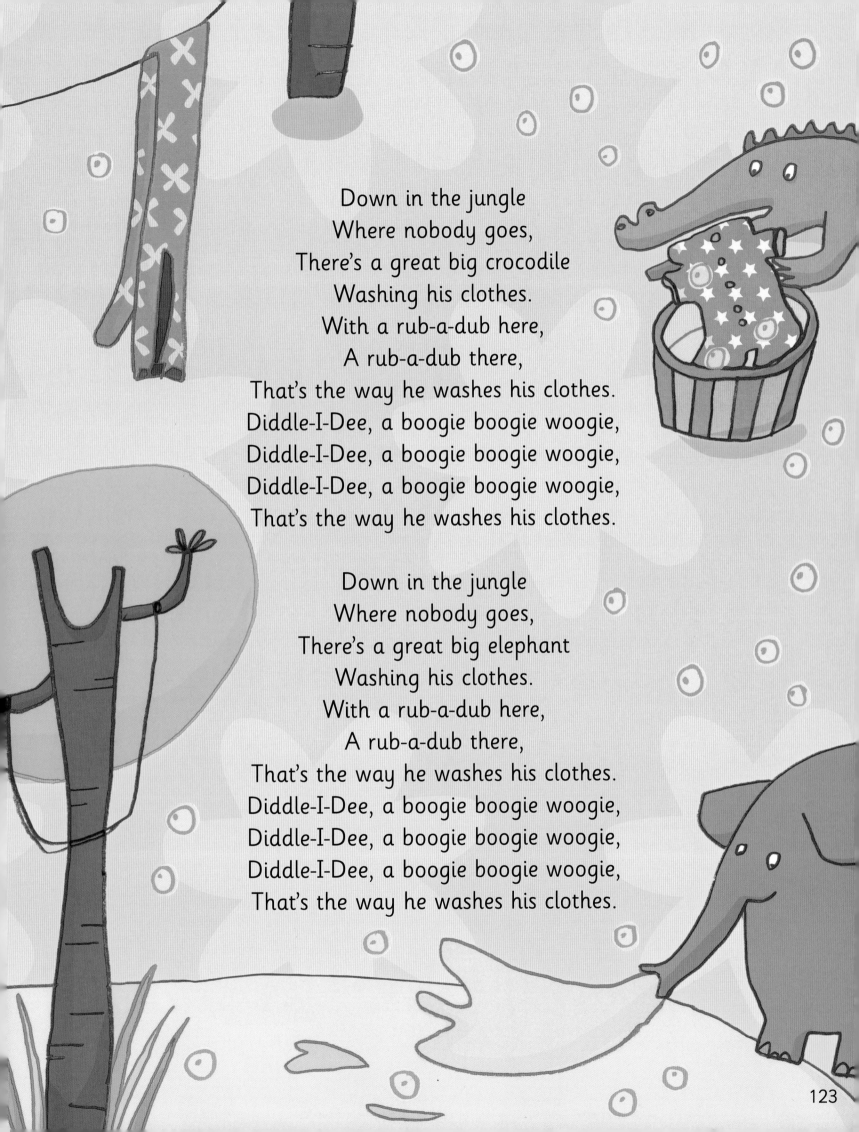

Down in the jungle
Where nobody goes,
There's a great big crocodile
Washing his clothes.
With a rub-a-dub here,
A rub-a-dub there,
That's the way he washes his clothes.
Diddle-I-Dee, a boogie boogie woogie,
Diddle-I-Dee, a boogie boogie woogie,
Diddle-I-Dee, a boogie boogie woogie,
That's the way he washes his clothes.

Down in the jungle
Where nobody goes,
There's a great big elephant
Washing his clothes.
With a rub-a-dub here,
A rub-a-dub there,
That's the way he washes his clothes.
Diddle-I-Dee, a boogie boogie woogie,
Diddle-I-Dee, a boogie boogie woogie,
Diddle-I-Dee, a boogie boogie woogie,
That's the way he washes his clothes.

Five Little Men in a Flying Saucer

Five little men in a flying saucer,
Flew round the world one day.
They looked left and right,
But they didn't like the sight,
So one man flew away.
Zooooooooooom!

Four little men in a flying saucer,
Flew round the world one day.
They looked left and right,
But they didn't like the sight,
So one man flew away.
Zooooooooooom!

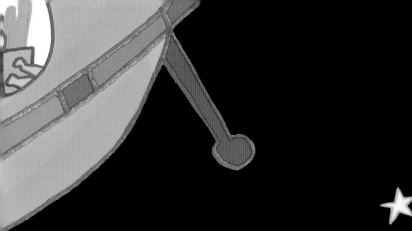

Three little men in a flying saucer,
Flew round the world one day.
They looked left and right,
But they didn't like the sight,
So one man flew away.
Zooooooooooooom!

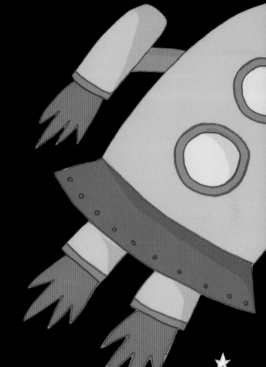

Two little men in a flying saucer,
Flew round the world one day.
They looked left and right,
But they didn't like the sight,
So one man flew away.
Zooooooooooom!

One little man in a flying saucer,
Flew round the world one day.
He looked left and right,
But he didn't like the sight,
So that man flew away.

ZOOOOOOOOOM!

Ten Fat Sausages

Ten fat sausages sizzling in a pan,
One went pop and the other went BANG!

Eight fat sausages sizzling in a pan,
One went pop and the other went BANG!

Six fat sausages sizzling in a pan,
One went pop and the other went BANG!

Four fat sausages sizzling in a pan,
One went pop and the other went BANG!

Two fat sausages sizzling in a pan,
One went pop and the other went BANG!

No fat sausages sizzling in the pan,
But all of a sudden the pan went BANG!

It went BANG! BANG! BANG!
Now there are no fat sausages
And no frying pan!

Jelly on a Plate

Jelly on a plate!
Jelly on a plate!
Wibble-wobble,
Wibble-wobble,
Jelly on a plate!

Candles on a cake!
Candles on a cake!
Blow them out,
Blow them out,
Candles on a cake!

Sweeties in a jar!
Sweeties in a jar!
Shake them up,
Shake them up,
Sweeties in a jar!

Sleeping Bunnies

See the bunnies sleeping till it's nearly noon.
Shall we wake them with a merry tune?
They're so still, are they ill?
Wake up little bunnies!
Hop little bunnies, hop, hop, hop.
Hop, hop, hop; hop, hop, hop.
Hop little bunnies, hop, hop, hop.
Hop, hop, hop...

See the bunnies sleeping till it's nearly noon.
Shall we wake them with a merry tune?
They're so still, are they ill?
Wake up little bunnies!
Skip little bunnies, skip, skip, skip.
Skip, skip, skip; skip, skip, skip.
Skip little bunnies, skip, skip, skip,
Skip, skip, skip...

See the bunnies sleeping till it's nearly noon.
Shall we wake them with a merry tune?
They're so still, are they ill?
Wake up little bunnies!
Jump little bunnies, jump, jump, jump.
Jump, jump, jump; jump, jump, jump.
Jump little bunnies, jump, jump, jump
Jump, jump, jump...

Hop little bunnies, hop, hop, hop,
Hop, hop, hop, hop, hop, hop.
Hop little bunnies, hop, hop, hop,
Hop, hop, hop!

The Farmer's in his Den

The farmer's in his den,
The farmer's in his den,
Eee-eye addy-oh,
The farmer's in his den.

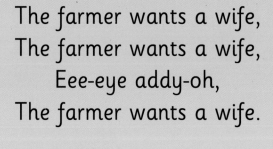

The farmer wants a wife,
The farmer wants a wife,
Eee-eye addy-oh,
The farmer wants a wife.

The wife wants a child,
The wife wants a child,
Eee-eye addy-oh,
The wife wants a child.

The child wants a dog,
The child wants a dog,
Eee-eye addy-oh,
The child wants a dog.

The dog wants a bone,
The dog wants a bone,
Eee-eye addy-oh,
The dog wants a bone.

We all pat the dog,
We all pat the dog,
Eee-eye addy-oh,
We all pat the dog.

130

One Finger, One Thumb

One finger, one thumb, keep moving.
One finger, one thumb, keep moving.
One finger, one thumb, keep moving.
We all stay merry and bright.

One finger, one thumb, one arm,
keep moving.
One finger, one thumb, one arm,
keep moving.
One finger, one thumb, one arm,
keep moving.
We all stay merry and bright.

One finger, one thumb, one arm, one leg,
keep moving.
One finger, one thumb, one arm, one leg,
keep moving.
One finger, one thumb, one arm, one leg,
keep moving.
We all stay merry and bright.

One finger, one thumb, one arm, one leg,
stand up, sit down, keep moving.
One finger, one thumb, one arm, one leg,
stand up, sit down, keep moving.
One finger, one thumb, one arm, one leg,
stand up, sit down, keep moving.
We all stay merry and bright.

Five Little Ducks

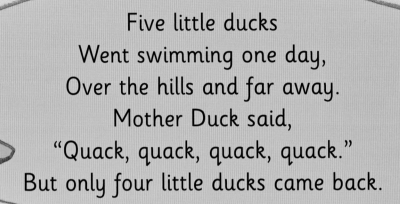

Five little ducks
Went swimming one day,
Over the hills and far away.
Mother Duck said,
"Quack, quack, quack, quack."
But only four little ducks came back.

Four little ducks
Went swimming one day,
Over the hills and far away.
Mother Duck said,
"Quack, quack, quack, quack."
But only three little ducks came back.

Three little ducks
Went swimming one day,
Over the hills and far away.
Mother Duck said,
"Quack, quack, quack, quack."
But only two little ducks came back.

Two little ducks
Went swimming one day,
Over the hills and far away.
Mother Duck said,
"Quack, quack, quack, quack."
But only one little duck came back.

One little duck
Went swimming one day,
Over the hills and far away.
Mother Duck said,
"Quack, quack, quack, quack."
And five little ducks came swimming back.

Baa, Baa, Black Sheep

Baa, baa, black sheep,
Have you any wool?
Yes sir, yes sir,
Three bags full.

One for the master,
One for the dame,
And one for the little boy
Who lives down the lane.

Here We Go Round the Mulberry Bush

Here we go round the mulberry bush,
The mulberry bush, the mulberry bush.
Here we go round the mulberry bush,
On a cold and frosty morning.

This is the way we wash our hands,
Wash our hands, wash our hands.
This is the way we wash our hands,
On a cold and frosty morning.

This is the way we wash our face,
Wash our face, wash our face.
This is the way we wash our face,
On a cold and frosty morning.

This is the way we brush our teeth,
Brush our teeth, brush our teeth.
This is the way we brush our teeth,
On a cold and frosty morning.

This is the way we comb our hair,
Comb our hair, comb our hair.
This is the way we comb our hair,
On a cold and frosty morning.

The Ants Go Marching

The ants go marching one by one.
Hoorah! Hoorah!
The ants go marching one by one.
Hoorah! Hoorah!
The ants go marching one by one;
The little one stops to suck his thumb,
And they all go marching down into the ground
To get out of the rain.
Boom! Boom! Boom! Boom!

The ants go marching two by two.
Hoorah! Hoorah!
The ants go marching two by two.
Hoorah! Hoorah!
The ants go marching two by two;
The little one stops to tie his shoe,
And they all go marching down into the ground
To get out of the rain.
Boom! Boom! Boom! Boom!

The ants go marching three by three.
Hoorah! Hoorah!
The ants go marching three by three.
Hoorah! Hoorah!
The ants go marching three by three;
The little one stops to climb a tree,
And they all go marching down into the ground
To get out of the rain.
Boom! Boom! Boom! Boom!

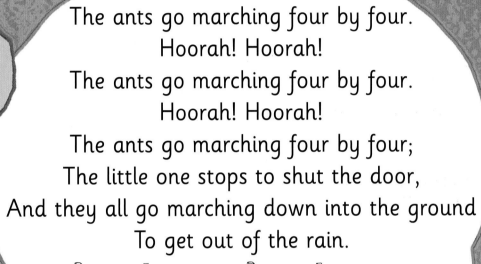

The ants go marching four by four.
Hoorah! Hoorah!
The ants go marching four by four.
Hoorah! Hoorah!
The ants go marching four by four;
The little one stops to shut the door,
And they all go marching down into the ground
To get out of the rain.
Boom! Boom! Boom! Boom!

The ants go marching five by five.
Hoorah! Hoorah!
The ants go marching five by five.
Hoorah! Hoorah!
The ants go marching five by five;
The little one stops to take a dive,
And they all go marching down into the ground
To get out of the rain.
Boom! Boom! Boom! Boom!

The Grand Old Duke of York

The grand old Duke of York,
He had ten thousand men,
He marched them up to the top of the hill,
And he marched them down again.

When they were up, they were up,
And when they were down, they were down,
And when they were only halfway up,
They were neither up nor down.

Humpty Dumpty

Humpty Dumpty sat on a wall,
Humpty Dumpty had a great fall;
All the King's horses and all the King's men,
Couldn't put Humpty together again.

Head, Shoulders, Knees and Toes

Head, shoulders, knees and toes,
Knees and toes.
Head, shoulders, knees and toes,
Knees and toes.
And eyes and ears and mouth and nose,
Head, shoulders, knees and toes,
Knees and toes.

Twinkle, Twinkle, Little Star

Twinkle, twinkle, little star,
How I wonder what you are.
Up above the world so high,
Like a diamond in the sky,
Twinkle, twinkle, little star,
How I wonder what you are.